Bea and Brodies' MINDFUL JOURNEY

featuring the art of Heather McLennan
and
the words of Susan Cohen

First edition, 2020
The Wee Book Company Ltd

The Wee Book Company

www.theweebookcompany.com

Art/illustration copyright ©Heather McLennan
Text copyright ©Susan Cohen
www.susancohen.co.uk

A catalogue record of this book is available from the British Library

ISBN 9781913237226

D1471410

Graphic design consultancy by www.colorprinz.com
Printed in Scotland by Bell & Bain Ltd, Glasgow

Brodie stood and looked up
At the cloudless bright blue sky,
He didn't feel so happy
But he wasn't sure quite why.

The honey bees buzzed round him
And tried to cheer him up.
'Bee happy!' they buzzed cheerfully,
'Think of life just like a cup,

A cup that's not just half full
But brimming to the top!'
'Scram! Vamoose!' cried Brodie.
Jings, he was in a strop!

Nae matter how the wee bees
Buzzed all about the place,
None would put a real smile
On Brodie's hairy face.

His thoughts were in a jumble,
He didn't know just how to be,
He turned his back on the braw day
And gazed straight out to sea.

His favourite bee buzzed over,
Little Bea was her sweet name,
'Don't waste the day, dear Brodie!
Och, that would be a shame!'

Bea had always had his heart
And he had hers right back,
Her energy would lift him up
And put him back on track!

For Brodie was a thinker
Whose thoughts tied him up in knots.
Not always but just sometimes,
Not much, not lots and lots.

'Now Brodie,' said wee buzzy Bea,
'Why don't we make a start
On the path to special places
Which warm and lift our hearts?

These places are in Scotland,
A place that we call home,
A place which lifts our spirits up
No matter where we roam.

With its cities and its castles
With its sandy island shores
With its villages, lochs and rivers
How could we wish for more?

This land has always been our strength
It's with us near and far,
It's our constant guiding light
Just like the great North Star.

They went first to Edinburgh Castle
And marvelled at its glory,
They looked at every ancient stone
And thought about its story.

Atop an extinct volcano,
An ancient royal home
To lords and ladies, kings and queens
And magical beasts who roamed

Round all the open spaces
That surrounded its high walls
And now are lush green parks
With fountains and waterfalls.

Bea and Brodie mindfully
Stood and stared and listened
To sounds round the old castle
Feeling sunshine as it glistened.

'Now,' said Bea, 'let's both go
To a place way up on high
Where we can see the city
Framed by the bright blue sky.

They found themselves on Calton Hill
Mid monuments of stone
And breathing in the clean clear air
Bea and Brodie felt alone.

Standing there together
Almost moved the friends to tears
For it let them see with fresh eyes
Their way ahead, so clear.

They felt so free that little Bea
Reminded her dear friend
That the day belonged to them,
A day like this should never end!

They went next to Dean Village
With its courtyards and its towers,
Its old walls made from sandstone
And its millstones turned by power

Of waters which flowed Northwards
All the way out to the sea
Waters said to wash your cares away
When you cast them in and let them be.

And so that's what the friends did
As they stood there side by side,
They let their cares go silently
And watched them slowly glide

'Til they floated out of sight
And more important, out of mind
'Now,' said Bea, 'best keep moving
Let's leave this special place behind

For Brodie, there is somewhere
Which I think you will agree
Is one of Scotland's most awesome sights
The whole world wants to see!'

Brodie quietly followed her
For Bea was always right,
And soon they found themselves
Standing bathed in warm sunlight.

Divided by the bright blue sea,
Capital city and Kingdom of Fife,
Bea and Brodie were speechless,
They were really living life!

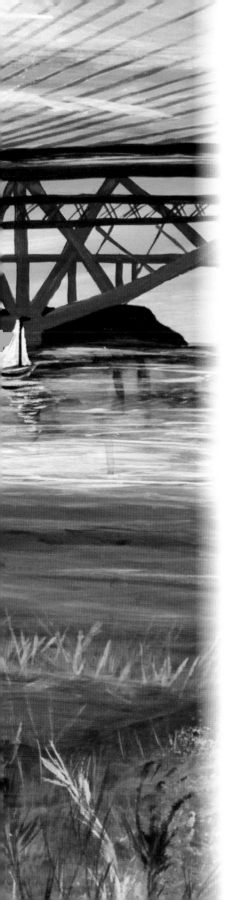

They stood upon a stretch of beach,
The wild free Blackness Sands,
And saw how the great Firth of Forth
Flowed deep into Scotland's lands.

They stared at the Three Bridges,
Each telling its own story,
Spanning seas with majesty,
Sun shining on their glory.

They marvelled at how the bridges
Were built and came to be
How they transported people safely,
An inspiring sight to see!

It made the dear friends happy
To witness such amazing sights
It inspired them to live fully
And raised their spirits to new heights.

Brodie felt so happy,
His mind was calm and clear,
Bea's love had revived him
So had Scotland, which he loved so dear.

It's a place of stunning beauty
Of friends – faithful, loyal and strong
It's a place where you can hear your heart sing
A joyous rainbow of song.

Good friends belong together
Every single day,
When one is feeling low and lost
The other can light the way.

Like Greyfriars Bobby and his master,
Bea is Brodie's heart
Brodie knows no matter what
They'll never be apart.

MORAG & MATTY

'Everything is energy
and energy is me'
Said a happy Brodie
To his loving little Bea.

'At times I feel a wee bit lost
My vibration needs a lift,
To know you as a darling friend
Is my life's most precious gift!

FLORA

HARRIS

BRODIE

HEATHER

FIONA

You remind me how to be
Alive right here right now,
I think a little honey bee should be
Assigned to every Highland Cow

To buzz lightly all about them
When they feel heavy and quite low
To help them get back on their hooves
And let everything just flow.

You've taught me to feel what surrounds me
And listen to sounds so bright
And smell the sweet smells of nature
And appreciate its beautiful sights,

You've taught me how to savour tastes
And use all of my senses,
You have helped remind me
Of just how brilliant life is!'

Bea and Brodie stood still and calm
Under their favourite tree
Mindfully using their senses -
How many can YOU see?

And so it was that Bea and Brodie
Headed home - their favourite place
Between the mighty ancient trees
Where they felt the calm and grace

Of nature in her glory
Of flowers in full bloom.
Be like Bea and Brodie
And you know that pretty soon

You'll learn to be all mindful
And careful with your thoughts,
You can make each day a good day
Instead of drawing lots

To find what mood you might be in
No, your mind makes it all real!
Live your life, be happy!
And know your own ability to heal.

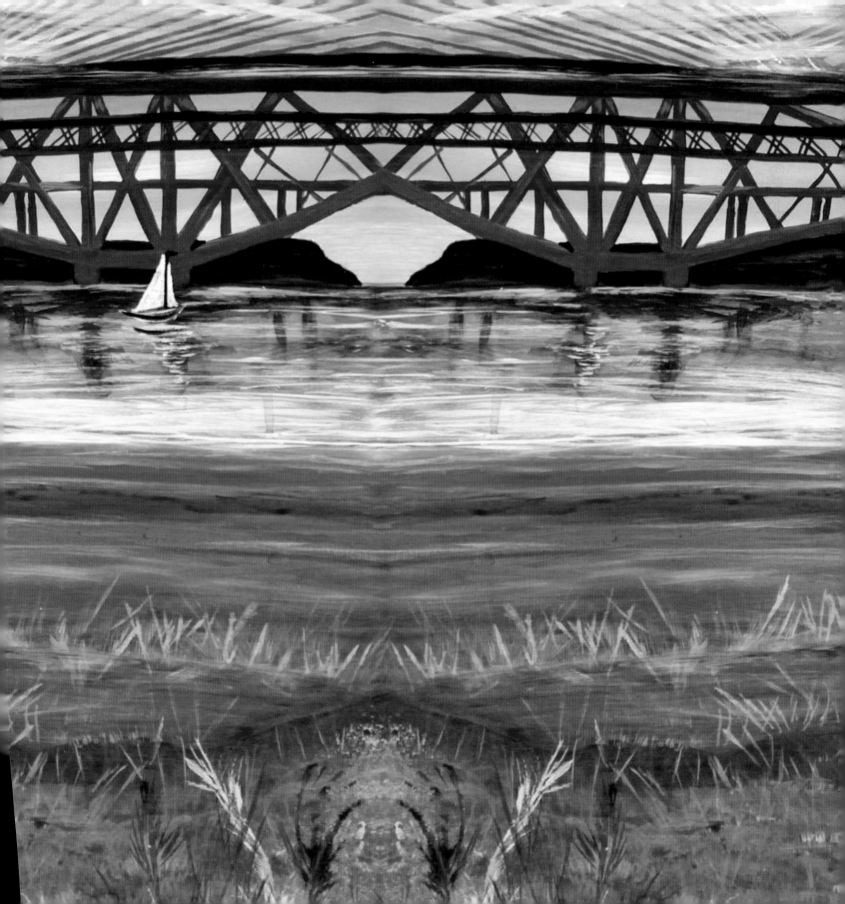

To purchase prints of illustrations appearing in this book and keep up with the latest adventures of Bea and Brodie, go to www.theweebookcompany.com

A donation is made to It's Good 2 Give from every book sale. This wonderful charity supports young cancer patients and their families through difficult times, and provides them with much-needed periods of respite and relaxation at its award-winning Ripple Retreat on beautiful Loch Venachar.

More information about the charity can be found at www.itsgood2give.co.uk